DEDICATION

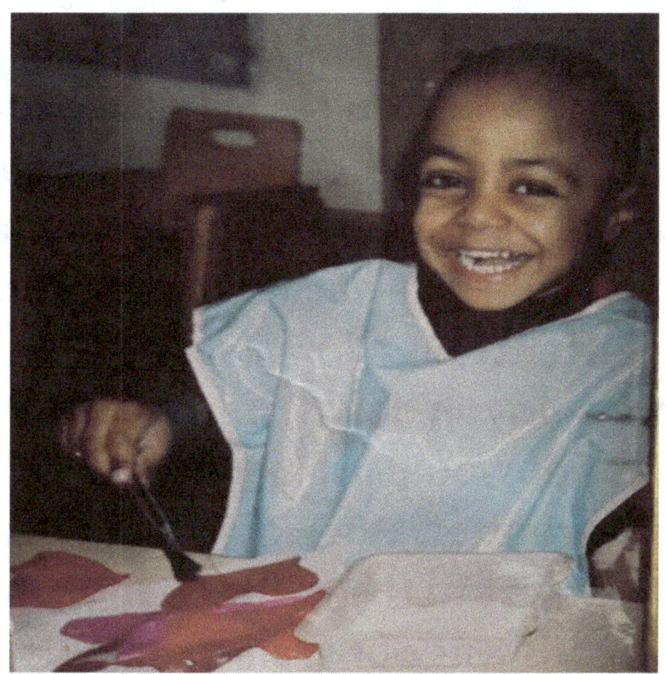

I have unconditional love for all my children. Dondi Jr., Kayla, Donovan. However, this book is dedicated to my son Mekhi Jose Burroughs. He spent the first few months of his life in the hospital as he was born prematurely. Numerous surgeries he had to endure as a result from near death experiences. He did pull through and is doing fine. He is and will always be my soldier and inspiration. This book is also dedicated to two very special people who are no longer here. My Great Great Grandmother Daniela Cruz who was and still a inspiration to me. She didn't speak any English and I always remember her sitting in the window of her brown stone on the 2nd floor in Bushwick Brooklyn. She would make sure that me, my siblings, and cousins were ok while we played as kids in front of the house. She would call us in and say, " Quires un poco de leche, do you want some milk, or, quires un poco de jugo, do you want some juice." After we drank the juice, she would give each of us a quarter ha-ha, hey, a quarter went a long way back then. Then we would run down the stairs and our grandmother would ask us the same thing and gave us a quarter. We would hall tail and run down the street to the corner bodega store and all we heard was our grandfather "Hey, Hey, Hey," wait for me, and he would walk us and just brag to all his friends about his grands in the store. It was surely a blessing to be able to have both you great great and grand mother and father. Peace and Blessings. January 3rd, 1903 to May 15th, 2003. And my good friend, my brother from another mother, Mr. Fred (Re-Run) Berry. Best known for his role as Freddie "Re-Run Stubbs," from the 1970's television show "What's Happening." March 19th, to October 23rd, 2003. I just want to mention that I met him in Flatbush Brooklyn at a friend of mines, Comedian Macio who had his annual block party. Rerun was with Pee Wee Dance, a icon, break dancer and Hip Hop

Historian. In our travels, we have spoken to thousands of youths. I want to say this because it was the funniest thing. He stayed with me periodically when I lived in Hamden Ct. I will never forget, one day I had to go to work and he was there, he decided to take my dog Recola for a walk, and I guess my dog seen a cat or something he said and Recola took off. He said he ran after Recola and finally got him. But the funniest thing. When I came home, my neighbor Mr. Charlie who is a good friend of mines who owns a bar called Chazmos in New haven Dix-well Ave, I had to give him a shout out ha-ha. Anyways, charlie came up to me and said, "Hey Dondi, maybe I was seeing things but I seen a heavy set guy, wearing a red barrette hat and he looked like Re-run and he was chasing after your dog." I said yes that was Rerun ha-ha. Him and Re-run became good friends after that and Re-run would hang out at Chazmos. Only once in a life time do we have or meet someone who holds a special place in our hearts. I was honored that he thought of me as a great friend as well and he gave me his red hat which I cherish. Peace and Blessings, my Brother Rerun.

ACKNOWLEDGEMENTS

I put God first for allowing me to be born and for opening up my eyes allowing me to see that better days were to come, but only on his time, not mines. I give love and thanks to my parents who raised us the right way and no matter what, always took the time to teach us, love us and made sure none of us went without. I love you both very much. Thank you, God, for giving me such wonderful parents, I give you all the thanks and glory.

To my sister and brothers whom I greatly respect and love. I first want to say that for the exception of me, and maybe my youngest brother, we were not musically inclined like my dad the rest of my siblings. Anthony, thank you for always looking out for us as the big brother. You have written and produced some of the most beautiful music that is on albums of great artists which can be heard all across the world. Binky, I always told you that you have a golden voice and should really take it to the next level, it's never too late, you been doing this since high school going to ECA, singing and doing plays. Bobby, ever since a young boy, you wanted to become a singer. I remember when we had family nights and I would just sit and watch you all and you use to watch Anthony and Binky sing while dad played the congas wearing his Dashiki ha-ha. Until you finally got your chance to show your skills, you started your R&B group Room Service, you made a few albums, traveled the world, worked not only with other artist but collaborated on several projects with different artist, and I even performed at the Worlds Famous Apollo Theater. All of your hard work and determination has paid off. Every time I hear the music you all have created on the radio, I just smile. But even more, you gave up that career so you could focus more on the more important things in life, like Family. I don't know too many dudes that would have done what you did. At least you can say you did it and accomplished your goals. No worries, in the years to come, you will be blessed even more for your efforts, trust. My brother Terrance. Although you really wasn't into the music scene, you always was present and supported the rest of the family. I am just as proud of you. You took on a position that not many people can do. You became a fire fighter, putting your life on the line for others. That takes a real dedicated person to do what you do, love you. To my other half, Dimas. Ever since we found out our grandmothers had the same last name of Cruz, we created a bond that could never be broken. We been through a lot in our times, good, bad, happy, sad. We laughed and cried together, several times we almost died together. Thanks for having my back and me having yours. Even though you always stepped in and wouldn't let me fight my own battles. Don't tell me I wasted all those years at Top Ten Karate hahaha. Just know that I love you Primo to the end. To Renee, my adopted sister. You have been apart of our family since we were kids. Thanks for all your support, and I commend you for all you do teaching sign language. To my mentor Mr. Jimmy Lee Moore. Ever since middle school being my teacher, you have always given me good sound advice. I truly value you as a great teacher and a great friend. To all my students who I haven taught and mentored through out the years. I consider all of you my children. Its funny, when I speak about my kids, some people ask me how many do I have, I just say, hundreds, and they look at me like I am crazy. Until you become a teacher or a mentor and create that bond and the student become apart of you, you will not understand. Even after they graduate, I still am apart of most of my student's life. To my 3 adopted daughters Quianna, Jasmine, Dominque,I love you very much. To Jamila, Leon,

Wilmont, Shana, Julio, and Jessica, Jasmine and Jessica, and all others who were and still apart of my life. To all my relatives, there are to many to name and thank, I care and love you all. I do want to give a special thanks to my cousins, Larry, Ingrid, Sherrie, Deb, and Unk Whirlee, all in Brooklyn. I appreciate all of you in assisting me with kicking off my Teens Only TV Show on Brooklyn's B-CAT, love you all. I really appreciate all the organizations and companies and clothing companies who have supported the show throughout the years. I think, well I know that I have received almost a million dollars' worth of clothing that I have given throughout the years to my students in the school system. A big shout out to all the schools in the New Haven, Hamden, West Haven district and Tri State areas where I have conducted workshops, and presentations. Special thanks to Hill House, Mr. Lyons and Joyce at the printing shop. (Teachers), Mr. Bob Davis, Mrs. Baldino, Mrs. Roberts. Principal, Mr. Garrise, thanks for showing love and support. To my drill team, the Foot Stompers, they can't erase what we were, we didn't need no drums, we still got busy, all of you are still number one in my book. Coach Tom Flemmings, Mr. Hunt, love ya. To my almamater Wilbur Cross, thank you for allowing me to come back to teach the UPI program, through Mr. Frank Crump and Tom Flemmings. The Hill Health center, Mr. Cornell Scott, you are an amazing person, love you my brother. Steve Ingrim, Lonelle Lawson, Domingo, Mildred. The entire crew at CTV for making the Teens Only Show its home base. Carol from Ct. Vibes, DJ Splash, Justice, who did the live taping of my first Teen Summit show on the New Haven Green, continue to do big things my brother. B WAK, DJ Stizz, TC Islam, Gottie in Atlanta, Pat Boozer, Surviving in the Hood,KOG, Dave Blackmon, Tim, Stacy who was one of my students and became my camera person and good friend. My C0-Host Anissa Hann, Julio Padilla, Jessica Means, Faye, Jasmine and Jessica AKA twins, and all the others who sat on the panel. I appreciate all of you. B-CAT in Brooklyn, Peoples TV in Atlanta GA. Polly T. McCabe Principal, Mrs Brenda Thomas, James and Hollywood, the Palace Theater, WYBC Juan and your crew for all your support. Neal and Paula at the Kangol Hat Company in NY for giving the show hundreds of hats for my students, they loved them, and I'm guilty, I kept one for myself ha-ha. To Jody, Denise, Gabriel and Serena at the Gale group in NY for all the Tees, jackets, and brand name clothing for my students. My good friend Beverly Harrise and the Mt. Zion Seventh Day Adventist Church for supporting the show.

The New Haven Job-corps Center for allowing me to speak and eventually landing a teaching position there. Mr. And Mrs. Coffield, Ann Marie from AIDS Interfaith for giving me a position and the chance as a outreach worker. D&S name plates. Comedians Flex, Talent, Terry Hodges, Arceneaux and Mitch, Macio, Mugga, Fig and Jimique. DJ Biz Markie, DJ Red Alert, Dave fresh, DJ Mario, Troy, Byrdy, Kenny Powell and others who have been there to support the cause. Brian from Ring One Boxing, Badd Chad Dawson, Larry Rogers Sr. And Jr. Top Ten Karate and Judo. Mike Jai White, thank you and Larry for supporting the show and taking time out to talk to my students and just being apart of the Elm City and working with our youth. Kingsly at Catchen Reck Records in Bridgeport for setting up all the interviews with all the rap artist at your store. Pee Wee Dance in Harlem, Julie Black, Deidre Gary from Visual Marketing, thank you both for setting up all the interviews and allowing my students to meet such influential artist. Ralph McDaniel's from Video Music Box, I appreciate seeing the video I was in with the rap group PHD and the song I'm Flippen, even though it was cut short because of the gun play and no longer able to be aired, to violent. DJ's Big Mike and his brother Boobie out of Brownsville BK, thank you for

DJ-ing our first annual Drug Awareness/ Stop the Violence program at IS 390 in Brooklyn, it was a success. Lee at Ujama Bookings, my boy and first rap artist reppen the Elm, Denny Den, Chazz at heavy Hitten Ent. Washington Heights, Gordon at broadcast Juice, MCA, RCA, Logic, BMC, Columbia, DVS/Interstream, Sony, Jive, Universal Records. My boy Bobby Yan for your support with the videos and interviews. Trust B, you are going places, watch and see. Sue Aitchison at WWE, thank you so much for all the years of support and supplying the show with hundreds of tees for my students. Max and Mike at Jimmy's Urban Wear. Thank you for supplying all the tees for our staff vs student basketball games. To my boy, Carl Payne AKA Cockroach on the Cosby Show. Thank you for all your support and I remember me my brother and Tom Tom and our Morgan State crew always going to Howard University where you and Puffy were attending to chill there, we had good times. Donald Morrison (BGB), you have surely been an inspiration, not only for the New Haven area but for me to continue your legacy keeping busy in our community. Donnell Green and Shonne Gibson who supported me with my show when we all worked together at Continuum of Care. Mitch (ski) at Red Marketing NY.

W Haven Federation Teachers Union, Pat Lucan, Pat Delucia, Matt Borenstain and Frank Carrano, thank you for all of your support with the show and in the schools. I cannot forget my dude Mr. Donald Carter who has been a big support with not only the show but also speaking with me in the schools and helping me to launch my reflective clothing wear by designing a few of the outfits. Last but not least, my Morgan State crew. Tom tom, Fonz, Darren, Doc, Tubbs, Mt. Vernon, Butts, Jojo, Jeanette, sun shine, and my girl Annette from Gilligans Island, I'm sorry, St. Thomas ha-ha. Those were the days. I truly thank you all for your support and just being a part of my life.

FORWARD

In the dialogue of the Ancient Greek Philosopher, Plato, there is a section called The Allegory of the Cave. An allegory is a symbolic story meaning that all the characters, situations and objects in the story stand for something or someone else. In this Allegory, there are people who are living in a cave who believe that shadows cast by their fire are reality. One individual, however, sees a glimpse of sunlight from above and begins to ascend to the light. At first, he is blinded and overwhelmed by the brilliance of the sun, but gradually his eyes become use to the abundance of sunlight symbolizing true knowledge and reality. Now, this pilgrim must make a choice, he must decide if he will continue his journey to a higher awareness alone or return to share his knowledge with those people still comprised by illusions. Dondi like this pilgrim in this allegory, has made his journey to a higher awareness. As you will see in this beginning of Dondi's story, he encountered many "shadows" that tempted him, distanced him and could have led him to an unsavory end. Dondi's glimpse of that higher light, a better life, called him to develop self-discipline and caution. These became the foundations for building his higher self-styled to be pleasant, sincere, personable and perceptive when in public service. I am very pleased that Dondi has chosen to share his life story with the world. This in itself will enhance his position as a positive role model for his journey toward the sunlight. Dondi will always have my highest regard. "Bob Paglia, The Movie Man

SOMETHING IN MY HEAD SAID "JUST DO IT"

I was confused, I went downhill, I didn't show it, I fell into a state of depression. My spirit was down, I started to give up on myself. I started thinking of ways to end my life. I don't drink nor do drugs, but that day I did go to the Liquor store and get a half pint of Vodka. Took a few swig's and I thought that shooting myself would solve my problems would be solved. I had a shot gun and said to myself the only thing to do was to load it, aim and pull the trigger. The shot gun had a long barrel. I put the end of the barrel in my mouth but couldn't reach the trigger, I put my finger on the trigger but couldn't put the barrel in my mouth. I found a string and tied it to the trigger, put the toe part of my sneaker in the string near the trigger and put the barrel in my mouth, closed my eyes, waited a few seconds, pushed down on the string and it broke. I tried it again and the same thing happened. I couldn't do anything but laugh. I laughed so hard I started crying, I already felt like I couldn't do anything right, even kill myself. I went to plan B, I had a hand gun in the house as well. Those firearms were not mines; I was just holding them temporarily for someone. I took the handgun cocked it back, put the end of the barrel in my mouth, closed my eyes, pulled the trigger and…………. Well, I guess you are going to have to continue to read my story to find out the end result, sorry.

THE BEGINNING

I got married to my first love at a very young age, 24. During our six-year marriage, we had our first born, Dondi Jose Jr. Things happen in relationships and unfortunately, we divorced in 1988. We both realized we were young and were not ready. It was disappointing. I just knew that our marriage was forever. I tried to play like I was ok but I wasn't, I was mad, confused and feeling down and just wanted answers. I didn't show any emotions, I was depressed, my spirit was down, I started to second guess myself. I did a lot of praying, I put my trust in God. Sometimes I had those down moments but kept Prov. 3-5 in my mind to continue to put trust in God. When I had those down moments, that's when it seemed the Devil would invite himself into my world, through my emotions. Just prowling around like a roaring lion, a hungry shark, just waiting to attack. I wasn't really motivated anymore. This is when Tom Tom played an important role in my life. Let me tell you about Tom, he was more than a friend, he's my brother from another mother. We grew up together and been close ever since. I remember as kids, we went to Ivy street school and he lived right behind the school and we would play kick ball for recess and when we were on the field, we would have someone kick the ball over our head and we would run and get the ball, and just run to the candy store, buy candy then go back ha-ha. He is the reason why I no longer have my job, I was making $22 an hour, and back then, that was great. Tom was enrolled in college at Morgan State in Baltimore. He would come back and forth from Baltimore to Ct. He was home on break, and he had to return, and he suggested that me and my brother Bobby go back with him for the week end just to visit and maybe I may like it and maybe take some classes, make a new start. We enjoyed it so much that we didn't want to leave but we went back to Ct. Tom called me Monday morning and said let's go back to Baltimore, I said I got to work, he said I already took care of that, he called my supervisor and said he was my father and said I was sick and would be out of work for a few days. We went back to Baltimore, set up shop, got a apartment, me and my brother found jobs and we went back to Ct; to get our stuff and we were out. Tom was in school, so he didn't work but his pockets always seemed to be filled with money ha-ha. Me and my brother were happy, we both needed a change, but I still felt emptiness inside. Even though me and my wife were separated and getting a divorce, I still had a newborn son. Tom understood my situation and felt that it wouldn't hurt to start over, get away for a while, regroup, get myself together and work on a plan. While working on my plan, we still had fun. Tom introduced us to his boys at Morgan State. We all would go to visit other colleges and one in particular was Howard University where a good friend went, Carl Payne who played cockroach on the Cosby show and Puff Daddy also attended as well. We used to hang out. I really enjoyed Baltimore and learned a lot about life. Besides living in Brooklyn and Ct. I really never been out of state like that, so the move was new and just learning how the people and the environment different. Even though I started feeling better about myself, I still felt I was missing something in my life, my purpose. I constantly prayed for guidance and for God to show me what my purpose was. I think we stayed in Baltimore for a year and a half, Tom was graduating, and he wanted to go to Virginia to open up a clothing store. We all decided to go back north, tom went to VA, my brother moved to New Jersey to pursue his singing career and I went to Brooklyn, my place of birth. While I as in NY, I really started thinking and making plans for my future. I was closer to Ct, which able me to see my son more. I started to question myself, what do I want out of life? What's my next step or venture. Those questions stayed in my head. I was staying with a relative, my uncle whirlee in East NY. He got me a job working with him at a meat factory and driving truck making deliveries. The good thing about working there was there was a club down the street called the Q club and I would just sit outside and watch all the nice cars go by. I knew that the job was just temporary. I know that God had something else in mind for me but for now, this was it. Being in that cold meat factory got my mind right. Me and my brother bobby kept in touch, he started a R&B group called Room Service and they were doing well. I felt that my turn was coming soon. Me and my Unk use to sit down after work and just talk about a plan, maybe starting a small business. Well, the restaurant business it was. After finding a place, Ribs & Bibs was open. We found a place in Queens on Rock-away Blvd. The good thing about this project was we were able to get discounts on the meats and supplies needed which cut the cost down and cutting out the middleman because we both did the prepping and cooking which helped to cut the cost of hiring someone to do the work. When I was in high school, I worked at the Holiday Inn as a dish washer then short order cook learning from the head Chef Frank Thomas who taught me how to prepare certain dishes then learning how to prep then became the first cook at age 18. So, I had the experience of preparing meals and prepping. We did well the first year, there were a few other food places that gave us a run. It was hard to keep good help and we didn't do a lot of advertisements, just word of mouth. We spent long hours a day which I didn't mind because I enjoyed cooking. I open up 9am and there till 12am. Lesson learned that you just cannot rely on your friends or some family to support you. It was an experience, and we learned a lot about the restaurant business. All's I have to say Unk, is they can't erase what we had, Ribs & Bibs forever.

THE VISION

I remember one particular birthday, I was going to hang out with a few friends, even though I don't celebrate it, we were just going to hang out just for a while if I wanted, they were on standby. I remember going into my closet to look for something to wear, it was about 1130pm. I sat inside the closet just looking for something to wear and I started thinking about life and crazy thoughts were going through my head. I've always had this premonition about dying by gunshot and dying on my birthday. I always stayed in the house and never wanted to to go in fear that I was going to die. Ever since I was young, I felt that way, why, I don't know, I just don't know. I never shared this with my family. When some people get to the point in their life when they don't care anymore, the attitude changes. I remember one day while I was driving in East NY, I had a lot on my mind and I cannot recall where I was driving to, but another driver was pulling out of a driveway and almost side swiped my car. I looked at him and just shook my head. I stopped at the red light and he pulled up next to me. He said, "what's your problem," I said, "you are the one who almost hit me." He got out of his car, I got out of mines, he said he was going to shoot me. Well, that made me angry, so as I walked towards him, he pulled out a 357 magnum and pointed it at my chest. I laughed and said, "wait a minute, let me take my shirt off, I don't want to get any blood on it, I just brought it." So, I took it off and sat on the hood of his car and told him I was ready to die. He looked at me and said I was crazy. He got in his car and began to drive off while I was still sitting on the hood. As I jumped, I just laughed. Now that's not normal. It was very clear I had some issues. I had no fear, my mind was fixed to not care, I was ok with dying. Back to the story. It was 1989, I really didn't want to go out, something was telling me to stay in. I felt safe, I actually fell asleep in the closet. I was awakened by a bright angel like figure. Now this figure was like a bright light that extended his hand towards me with a look of reassurance. As soon as I took his hand, it seemed as if we were flying over the city. Everything was moving real fast. Colors were zooming by and all of a sudden, things came to a halt. I looked down inside of what appeared to be a hall, church, or a community center which was packed with people. I looked at the angel and he pointed down wards as if I should look more closely. I noticed that the majority of people there were teens and younger ones. As I glanced towards the front, I noticed my family, relatives and close friends there and my mother was crying. I seen myself in the coffin. It didn't bother me so much that I was deceased, I couldn't understand why so many teens were present. I turned back towards the angelic figure for answers, and it was gone. That's when I woke up finding myself still in the closet in a cold sweat. Seeing it was just about day light, I knew I had spent most of the night in the closet. That day, I called my parents like I always did, and I told my dad about my dream. I am very thankful to have parents who love and care so much about their kids. Like most parents, you may not like what you hear, and if your child expresses that he or she wants to end their life, of course they will be concerned. My parents always showed concern. They seemed to focus a little more on me because I was the quiet one. I sat back and just observed and watched things from a distance. When I talked to my dad about my dream, he explained to me that God was showing me my worth, and that I need to hang on because it looks like you are going to be doing something with youth. He also told me that God wants me to rely on him and continue to pray for guidance and strength. I did just that. I am so thankful I have parents who love and care so much about their kids. I was puzzled as to why so many youths were at my funeral to support me and my family. Maybe my dad was right, maybe God was showing me something, but what? I was not working with any youth at the time, although I've always seemed to have a positive effect when I spoke to youth. I would take time to listen and talk to them, not at them. Giving positive advice. Sometimes, that's all a teen wants, someone to listen as they vent and express themselves. I still resided in Brooklyn, I started thinking more on adjusting my life and what I needed to do. I have a cousin by the name of Ingrid. Ingrid is a police officer who worked for the 77th precinct in Brooklyn. We always talked about different ways on how to have more productive programs for our youth and how they can better themselves in the community. Also, ways that she could make a difference as a Police Officer. During one conversation, she said that I should focus on doing speaking engagements to talk the youth. She suggested I put together a program and have celebrities come and speak to the youth. We could focus on Gangs, Guns and Violence, Suicide, Teen pregnancy etc. She told me her precincts youth division was working on a similar program and I could assist and help with the program. After months of planning, we did kick off its first Drug Awareness Stop the Violence program at I S 390 in Brooklyn. The students really enjoyed having the celebrities there to talk to them. The students seen the police officers as regular people and not cops. As the celebrities arrived, the students were in the classroom windows yelling and screaming the celebrities' names and applauding. I even got a few claps ha-ha, it felt really good to know we are not only reaching our youth but trying to make a difference. We had the pleasure to have radio host Ed Lover, Dr. Dre, DJ Red Alert, Rappers KRS1 and his wife Mrs. Melody. Let me say that KRS1 is a excellent speaker and motivator, just listening to him motivated me to want to do more events and to speak, I was Hyped. Ralph McDaniels from Video Music Box showed love and dropped knowledge and positive words. We had local up coming artist to perform, I had a few relatives that DJ provide the music, Big up to Big Mike and his Brother Boobie. A few of the high ranked officers spoke and the best part is that the students listened. I mean you could hear a pin drop. There were at least 200 students who all gave their undivided attention and showed respect. I know the students will remember that day for years to come. Shout out to the 77th and all who attended and supported the cause, job well done. A few months went by and my mind was on a roll. Thinking on how I could do another event or even working for a organization helping youth. I would still go back and forth to see my son as he was getting older. He would also come and spend time with me. One visit to Ct. I met up with a friend who worked for the Hill Health Center community Clinic. I was introduced to Mr. Steve Ingram, the supervisor over the AIDS Outreach Program. I told him about the event I put together in NY. He said that would be great if we could do something like that here, but he didn't have any positions available. I said I was still living in NY but would consider re locating if a position becomes available. He said I should think about volunteering and getting my feet wet and once a position opens up, he would contact me, we could use a person like you. I thought about it and re located back to Ct. I was a little hesitant, I felt that people would look at me as a failure and say," Oh he's back, he couldn't make it out there." Do I regret leaving New Haven, no, I'm glad I took time off for myself. Now that I think about it, it was God's plan. Yes, I came back but doesn't mean failure. I stepped out on faith. I may have made a few mistakes along the way, but isn't that all part of life and growth? Dew to imperfection, we will make and continue to make mistakes, that's between you and God, not for man to judge? I eventually landed a position as a Health Education Outreach worker at the Hill health Center. I began to build a reputation within the community and schools. I received many invitations to speak at various schools and organizations thru out Ct. At Detention centers and special events. I am proud to say that I was apart of establishing the first school-based clinic in New Haven at Jackie Robinson Middle School. We called it the Body Shop. Me and my coworker Anissa Hann who came aboard the Hill Health Center. The school based clinic was a place where students learned about health education, we held classes and sessions using interactive methods and role play involving subjects like Teen Pregnancy, STD's, HIV/AIDS,Gangs, Guns and Violence, dropout prevention and more. We were able to teach, listen and make referrals. I want to go back to my coworker Anissa for a minute. She is Caucasian and one of the coolest Italian you ever want to meet. We were called "salt & pepper." One of her famous words was For getta bout it. At first, I was not sure if she would fit in or even last because most of the schools, we serviced were predominately African American, or Hispanic, but she pulled it off. The female students felt comfortable talking to her about personal issues. When we entered the schools, she was greeted warmly by the students. Back to the Body Shop, we raised money by putting on local talent shows so that we could raise money for positive trips. Our first big trip was to the famous Apollo Theater in Harlem NY. The tour was conducted by a good friend of mines, Mr. Billy Mitchell, and comedian Macio, who took time out of his busy schedule to speak to the students. We also took the students shopping at the 125 street Mart and we ate at the famous Sylvia's restaurant where the students had the pleasure of meeting Rev. Al Sharpton, and Jesse Jackson and they both even took the time to say a few words to our students. Most of the students have never even been to NY or the Apollo Theater. We had to limit the number of students participating in the body shop. It became so popular that parents were calling the school so that their child could participate in the program. There was actually a waiting list. I am proud to have been a part of establishing the body shop. All the students have learned so many things of importance and able to talk about the issues that they deal with every day. Me and Anissa wrote several mini grants to create after school programs that enabled the students to learn more about the things, they have concerns about. One grant allowed us to do a Teen Summit on the New Haven green. Connecticut Television taped the show, big ups to Justice for doing the taping. We held discussions on Substance Abuse, HIV/AIDS, Teen Pregnancy. Each participant had a Teen Summit tee shirt, and not only that, they all earned a stipend for participating. We received good reviews from the media and the community. That event opened up many more doors for us. We were doing more presentations at other Correctional facilities, and schools in other cities. It felt good to know we were making a difference. Anissa left the Hill Health Center, moving on to other opportunities and started working at AIDS Inter faith Network. I was a little disappointed, sad, but I was also happy for her. She told me once she was in, she would bring me in. She did just that, a year later, we were side by side, salt & pepper.

INTRODUCTION
TO THE
TEENS ONLY TV SHOW

I was asked to be a Co Host on a morning show that was very popular on CTV, called "The Morning Show." This show talked about Political Issues, hosted by Mr. Jim Martino. This was the beginning of something great to happen. I did the show as a co-host for several months and I had the idea of producing my own show. I spoke to a few of the producers who had show's and talked to them about my concept of doing a show that focused on the issues that teens face each day. After a few months of planning and preparation, I came up with the name Teens Only. I had to first take classes to be certified as a producer. I produced and hosted my first live call-in show and Anissa was my co-host. I continued the Morning Show which allowed me to expand my guest list for my show. All of this started in 1994 with the teens only show. I wanted to do a show that dealt with teens. One of my good friends, I consider him a brother from another mother, TC Islam who already had a teen show on CTV and I was so taken away by the way he was able to gather so many teens from the different areas in

New Haven, put them all on one stage and talk, no fights, no beef, no arguing. That I felt was Awesome. Our show received great reviews and even making the front page of the New Haven register. Our topic was Aids Education. I feel we have opened the door for those youth who are crying out for help. We began producing monthly shows. Our program became so popular that we received request to do a weekly show. That put the pressure on to really work on topics and to get guest for the show. All this while we were still working our regular schedule as outreach workers. We even had local talent to perform giving them as my good friend Rerun would say, "15 minutes of fame." They were able to perform as long as it was clean, no cursing. One show we had the honor to have from MTV Ms. Serina and Ms. Vivian from CNN who came to New Haven to do a story on "illy," weed lased with embalming fluid or PCP. All this made possible by my good friend Dr. Brewer from Yale New Haven Hospital. One of my favorite shows was called "Is rap music safe to listen too." my good friend and also one of my brothers from another mother, Actor/ Martial Artist, Michael Jai White who was on the panel who dropped knowledge to our teen guest. Sometimes we changed our show format if we received information on a shooting or a suicide and we would do the show to support that family. This also gave our viewers the opportunity to call in which helped us to build a relationship with the community. Since I started in 1994, I have produced over three hundred shows. At first, I thought that people wouldn't like or except my show because it was not on a national level, but when I was out, people would stop me and say, "hey, you the guy from the teens only show," and gave me compliments. I worked a part time job at a clothing store in the Milford Post mall and I will never forget the time when a young couple was standing in the front of the store at the door and was just looking at me, I was like oh boy, what did I do. They worked their way in and walked towards me and the guy said, "hey, you're name Dondi," I said yes, he said, me and my girl seen you and she said that's the guy Dondi from the teens only show, I said nah, can't be, what's he doing working here, so we had to find out. He said, "you have a real job," I said yeh and started laughing, I said I thought I was the only one who watched the show. They said we both watch it all the time, it was a pleasure to meet you sir. I thanked them, that meant a lot to me. As time went by, I received more compliments from students and parents who said they watch the show and how much of an impact the show had on their kids. It felt nice to know that people really recognized us as advocates. We received letters, awards and honored for our positive work. It didn't matter that our shoe was not on a national level, we actually loved being apart of the CTV family. We continued to push harder, helping our youth. Sometimes, we really don't know how much of an impact we have on a person. To the world, that student may not mean a thing, but to that one person, it may mean the world? Just to show how much of an impact we had on some youth, it actually saved me one night from getting shot. One night, I remember going to an ATM, as I stood there, I heard footsteps walking up towards the back of me and a voice said, "give me your money." I immediately put my hands up in the air and started laughing. I said, "I just came to see if I was over drawn, I didn't come to get any money." I lied but it worked ha-ha. He said, "Wait a minute, you sound like the guy from the teens only show. "I turned around, said, "that's me." He said he was sorry, if he knew it was me, he wouldn't have tried to rob me. I said, "can I put my hands down now," he said oh yeah, I'm sorry. I started talking to him and told him I could help him with a job or something, I didn't want to see him end up dead or in jail. I also said it takes one second to pull that trigger, and that will get you 100 years. He had a mask on so I couldn't see his face, but I could tell he was a little embarrassed. He put his gun in his coat pocket and said I'm straight, put his head down and walked off real fast. Thanks Teens Only Show, I didn't die that night, thank you God for watching over me.

GOING SOLO

Anissa moved on from AIDS Interfaith while I stayed for another year. I have to say that working with our clients has made me more sensitive and appreciative of life and the value it holds. I took on a few more task within the community. I became a member on a few boards like JUNTA, a Spanish based community program in the fair haven section. The CPG which worked closely with several health organizations. I served as the Secretary for CTV which enabled me to maintain a connection with many agencies when any referrals were needed, plus, I learned how the financial structure of how monies are allocated within the organization. I continued to do the show but added more co-host. Julio and Jessica who were students at Career High School at the time and Faye who were part of the teens only family, they got the chance to be apart of the show before Anissa left. They caught on fast and did very well holding it down. A lot of parents are the Do as I say, not as I do. This can be a little confusing because if a child sees an adult engaging in something that's not right, they say, why do they do it? No longer can we say that because as parents, we must lead by example because our children are looking for that positive direction, good values, good morals. With Anissa no longer on the show, it was just me, Julio, and Jessica and Faye who was a little older which made it a little more comfortable when dealing with the parent to help with those single families with the moms only, or dads only to just assist with not telling them what to do but offering our assistance with what we know. Was it easy, no, sometimes I would encounter a parent who felt intimidated because we were the out siders, but we always reassured them that we are just advocates sharing information that will hopefully fill in the gap of communication between the parent and child.

BEING WATCHED

People use to come up to us all the time and say they enjoy the show. Some say its informative, it's funny, and some say they even cry when we talk about sensitive subjects. Some say how we keep it real, no sugar coating. I am not ashamed to say that I do not have the answers to everything, but I do tell my callers that by the next show, I will have the answers to their questions, I just don't want to give inaccurate information. Some parents they enjoy the show and watch it with their kids. Our caller support is growing every week. I am asked every once in a while, how far am I going to take the show. National would e nice, but I must say that I am hooked on Public TV Access. I want to expand the show to different cities. Even if I never make it to that national level, I'm happy that I am able to still reach as many as we have. I want people to feel like the show is there show, a community show, plus my viewers are able to call in and express their views, which makes them feel a part of the show. Can't get that happiness on National TV. I truly thank you all for the love.

RESPECTED BY ALL

Its nice to see all of my students who have been on the show, either as host or to perform. Even those who have graduated went to college and came back to still be a part of the show, thank you. I remember I was at Wilbur Cross High School checking on a few students and one student walked up to me while I was talking to a few teachers and counselors. She said she needed to speak to me, it was important. I stepped to the side and she said she wanted to drop out of school because she thinks she is pregnant. After we talked for a while, we walked to the school-based clinic and spoke with the provider and counselor. I felt good about her wanting to only talk with me, out of all the people standing there. The next day when I went back to check on her, she said she was not pregnant and she took my advice to stay in school and to use protection, or to just abstain? I told her I appreciate her coming to me, that's Respect. Another time, I was at another school and a student came up to me, I think she was a freshman and she said she wanted to be on the show. I gave her the pager number for the show and told her to first get permission from her parents and let them know I will be calling to talk to them. Later on that day, I received a page from her, I called and her father answered the phone and I said hello, before I could explain or say who I was, he he started flipping out on me, shouting, "who are you and why are you calling here, my daughter is only 15." The student cried out, "dad, I think that's Mr. Dondi from the teens show, I told you he was going to call." There was a moment of silence then he said, he was sorry, he was just being a dad. He said he had to be careful now a days. He said he enjoyed the show and thanked me for taking the time out for his daughter. He even expressed that he was having a hard time communicating with her about boy issues. He said he is old school and do not believe in early dating. <u>That's Respect.</u> I have earned great Respect by all those who have worked with me, those who have watched the show, and in the school system. I thank you all.

THE PURPOSE
AND
READING BETWEEN
THE LINES

I just want to take you back to the beginning of my story when I sat in the closet and had that dream because every beginning has and end. That experience during the night I fell asleep in the closet changed my life. Back then, I didn't understand what my father was trying to tell me when he said, "God is trying to tell you what you are worth, by showing you what he did. "back then, I was not working with any youth, so I couldn't understand or even picture working with teens. I thought that I was ok with everything until I once again, I fell into another state of depression, even though I was doing positive things, I had relationship issues and it got the best of me. The dream was 1989, now 1998? Once again, I reached out to my parents, like always they ask how I'm doing, I said I was tired and they said try and get rest. I said I wasn't sleepy, just tired. I wanted to just say I didn't want to live anymore but it wouldn't come out. When a person is crying out for help, they may not come straight out and directly say they want to commit suicide, it's all just a mind game people play. They want you to put together the puzzle and hopefully the person will before it's too late. Off and on, I was ok, then not ok and one day, I went into a deep depressed mode, I don't drink or do drugs, but I went to the liquor store and got some fire water as the Indians would call it. I went back to the house, took a few sips, man that vodka was so nasty, I don't see how people can drink it, anyways, I started thinking about my life and I was just tired of doing for everyone and caring so much about people. I said to myself, or something said to me, well, you did what you could, hey it's time to end your life, just do it and get it over with, Do it. Like I said in the beginning, I was holding a few firearms for someone who was kind of going through some things and didn't want them in their home. The more I drank the easier it felt for me to end my life. I tried using the shot gun but that was unsuccessful. I took the handgun cocked it back, took another drink, put the barrel in my mouth, closed my eyes, put my head back, counted to 3, pulled the trigger and it clicked but made a funny sound because it jammed up. I still had the end of the gun in my mouth and said to myself in a low mumble," aint this something." I pulled it from my mouth, looked at the gun, it looked like the bullet went halfway into the barrel and jammed, I could see the bullet stuck. I pointed up ward, pulled the trigger and BAMMM, it went off. I just froze. I really got a reality check. It wasn't my time; the punk came out of me and I started crying and I unloaded both fire arms and locked them back up. After I got myself together, I did call my dad again to talk. I didn't tell him everything, but I told him that I just didn't have the desire to live anymore. What my dad told me next put the whole puzzle together. He said, "son, I just want to ask you a question, what are you doing with your life right now." I said I'm working. He said OK, doing what. I said I'm working in the schools teaching, I have the TV show, I got the mentor program, the drill team, he said stop right there. You see, that dream you had years ago when you fell asleep in the closet. I said you remember that he said yes. He said God was showing you to hang on, you have a purpose, and he has a plan for you that's going to be real powerful in the days to come and it involves working with youth. He said, all the things that you are doing now involves kids, teens. And remember at your funeral, what did you see, hundreds of youths right, so all those kids are the kids of today. God was trying to show you and tell you to hang on because you will be helping hundreds of youths. So, if you were to end your life, all those kids you seen at your funeral will e the same ones that will be there this time if you take your life. And also think about this, some of those kids may e going through rough times where they may contemplate suicide and they may say, I'm going to do what Mr. Dondi did and take my life? So you see, God has a plan and still does for you son, he's a powerful God and you need to continue to rely more on him in order to continue to be protected. My dad gave me Prov. 3-5 like he always does to trust in God and not rely on my own understanding. Now I see the Vision and realize what my dad was explaining to me. He helped me to understand how important life is, not just for me, but also for others. He wanted me to see how precious we are to God. I will always remember this experience and never forget everything my dad said which I feel God was talking to me through him. Its not like back in the biblical times where people heard voices from heaven. This is why I felt I needed to tell my story to the world, and for those who are going through the same thing, and hopefully by reading my story, that person will rely on God and all those he will put in place as his advocates, his voice. Suicide is not the answer. Never put yourself in a situation where you are alone when you are going through problems. Place yourself around people who you can talk to and that care for you and talk about what you are going through.

Don't think you're to much of a man or woman to ask for help. If you have to cry, go ahead and cry. At least you will live to see another day and be loved. I prayed and thanked God for stopping what could have been a tragedy. I try not to think that way anymore. We are not perfect and as much as we pray, there still may be times when we fall weak. When I feel myself falling, I continue to pray, putting trust in God. We often tend to become magicians trying to fool everyone, but the only one getting fooled was me. In order to love life, you have to live life first. In order for God to help you, you must help yourself first. Trust me, the storm doesn't last long, you will look back on all you went through because God is going to show you and give you direction and open up doors and you will be glad you didn't give in to the Devils trap. God willing, I will write my part two to this story and call it from the closet to the stage. Based on me sitting in the closet falling asleep and my story starting from there and where I am 20 years from now. Peace and Blessings, Love you all, God Bless.

QUOTES

"It has been a pleasure working with Dondi. He has demonstrated a commitment to the total community. This young man has many characteristics that make him outstanding. I am impressed with his persistence with and dedication to our youth. He has clearly shown the initiative required to make a difference."
Ms. Wanda Y. Gibbs, Principal Riverside Academy

"Dondi is a light in the pathway for our youth today. A lot of them are blinded by the darkness of the path that they walk on. He is truly a leader and is just as good of a motivational speaker as I am. Dance Monkey Dance."
Fred Re-Run Berry

"As an advocate for the teen community, Dondi's dedication and devotion can be measured by his willingness to put the issues addressed to the teens of today. The teens only show is a local popular television program that should remain a vehicle for teens to focus on and connect. We at CTV wish this type of program could sustain a weekly slot; not just for teens, but future teens and post teens. Dondi lets the teens voice be heard. His aspirations for moving forward socially

and with entertainment are aimed at our heroes of tomorrow......... our teens."
Dave Blackmon Assist. Manager CTV

"I met Dondi Burroughs in 1994, when I first came to Hill House High School as an administrator and coach for the boys basketball team. I first saw him on his TV show, and was very impressed with his professionalism as a commentator and host. What impressed me more was his strong proactive commitment to the youth in New Haven. Dondi presented a "lay it on the table" format in his show looking for real dialogue to real issues that affect our young generation. More importantly, his commitment to real solutions is what make this young man an outstanding role model citizen in our community. May God continue to Bless you, Dondi, in your work."
Tom Fleming, Administrator Hill house High

"Dondi is a people person who has been blessed with interpersonal skills that are uniquely blended with charm, grace and humility, which fills a room,"
Edward Cocchiola, Hill house High

"I've seen so many positive changes in your life within you and outside of you for all you give to your friends, your family and your community, especially the teens. It is an honor and a privilege to know you. With love and Blessings."
Attorney Joy Bershtein

"God's word is a lamp to light up our path to take on life's journeys. Dondi is a lamp that God uses to brighten many pathways for youth and families. I've seen him in action constantly helpful and deeply inspirational."
Deborah Salters, Mothers for Justice/Author

"I have known Dondi for over eight years. He has always had the children's best interest in mind. He looks for the positive in our youth. This brother's message is serious."
Harold J. Haughton, II, Wilbur Cross High Teacher/Coach

"I consider myself fortunate to call Dondi my friend. I couldn't be more proud of his dedication to young people. Watching Dondi is like watching magic. Dondi is what child advocacy and public service should be about. He is a true educator."
Jerry Baldino, Educator

ABOUT THE AUTHOR

Dondi Burroughs moved from Designing reflective wear for those who ride motorcycles, to the classroom, auditorium, television producing and hosting the Teens Only TV Show which is aired in Connecticut's CTV, Brooklyn's B-CAT, and Atlanta's People's TV. He began over 10 years ago as a community outreach worker and health educator. He moved into mentoring and teaching life and social skills dealing with the everyday issues teens go through. His cool urban approach prepares young audiences to receive the knowledge and experiences he brings. He acts as liaison representing "old school" parents helping them to communicate to their children. He serves communities giving countless hours, volunteering in the public-school systems, served on local boards and hosts an annual fundraising events. Becoming and Author was the next step in his life that seemed inevitable.

gallery

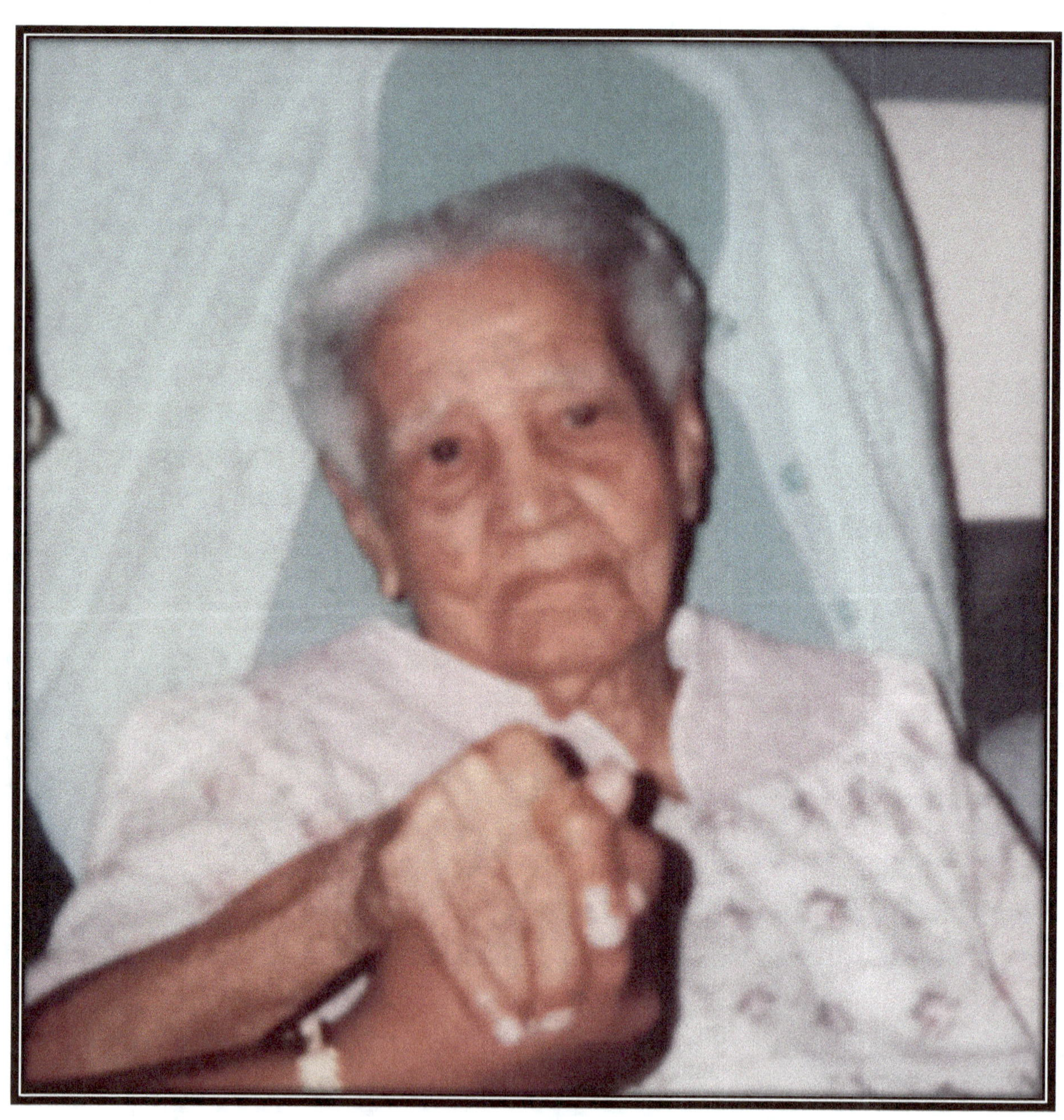

GREAT GREAT GRAND MOTHER

This is where it all began in Brooklyn as kids

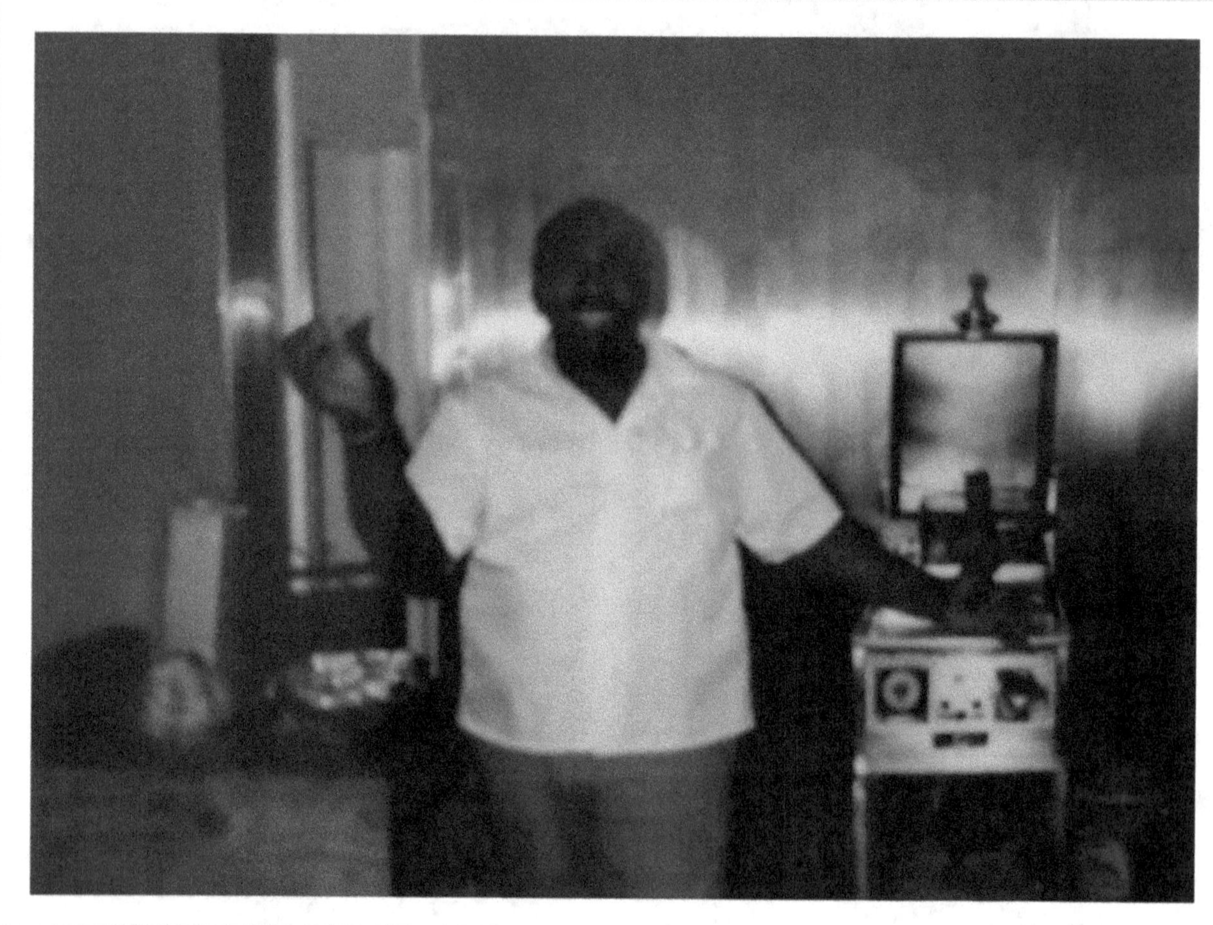

Unk Whirlee tasting his creations at Ribs & Bibs

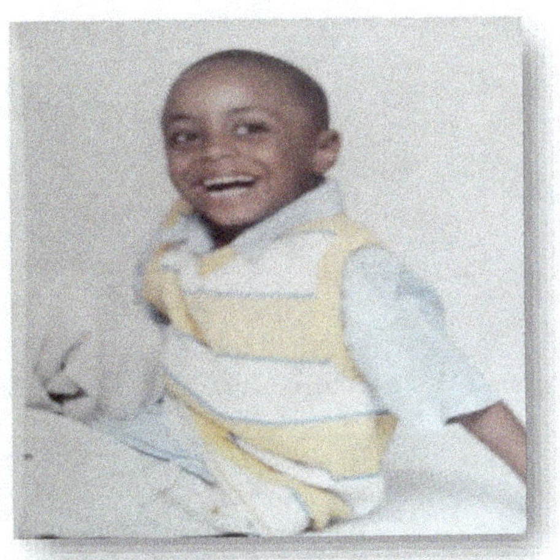

My son Mehki a few years later after being in hospital he is doing fine

My son Mehki and Donovan

Brooklyn's B-CAT Public TV

Me and Mr. Baldino with our children from Edgewood School

Teens Only Basketball event Tee shirt give away

My Brothers Bobby and Anthony in the limo on way to perform

Rev. Jesse Jackson who took the time to talk to my students at Sylvia's Restaurant Harlem NY

Ms. Wanda Gibbs with her students from River Side during the Teens Only student vs teacher Basketball game

Acon Interview

Carl Payne

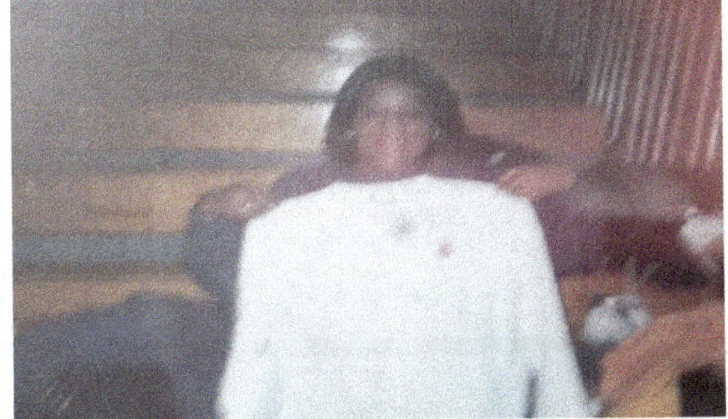

Ms. Gibbs got her a Tee

My boy Badd Chad Dawson took time to speak to my students at Jobcorps

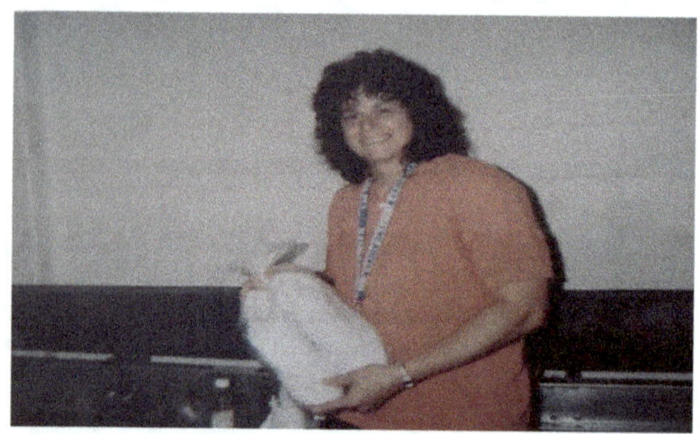

Sneaker give away to my students at Hillhouse

Receiving a certificate for speaking

My Jackie Robinson Crew rocking there hats

My students from Jackie Robinson Middle School sporting the Kangols

Staff vs Student Basketball game

Atlanta GA, I keep it moving

ATL

On set with my girl Judy and her crew of students

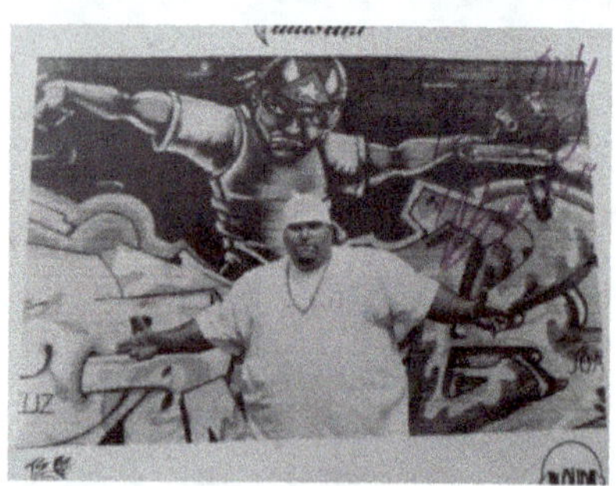

Big Pun. I asked him if he was a role model for our youth. He said no, because I still run the streets, I'm a inspiration for them to become a rapper and stay out the streets.

My Foot Stompers
Hillhouse High School

Allure

Edgewood School Crew

Mike J White at Hillhouse
to speak to my students

Comedian Terry Hodges took time to host our talent show given by AIDS Interfaith

On set
Teens only Tv Show

In NY with DJ Red Alert and Rerun

RIP my Brother, I will cherish this hat you gave me for ever

Fred "Rerun" Berry

My boy Ralph New Edition

Sticky fingers Onyx

On set

Taking a break from the show

Mobb Deep

Craig Mack Interview

Tee shirt give away Atlanta

My Morgan State Crew

My Brothers group Room Service

Morgan State Crew

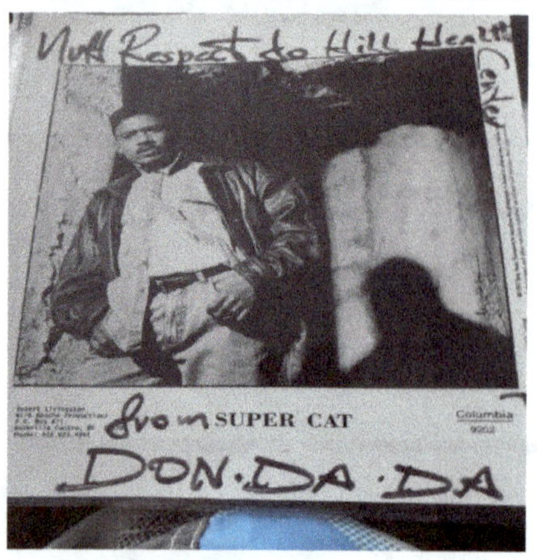

I was featured in this magazine, Don B Reflective Wear

Don B Tee Shirt

I have to Rep Teens Only

JR Crew

My boy Dave, thank you so much for everything love ya

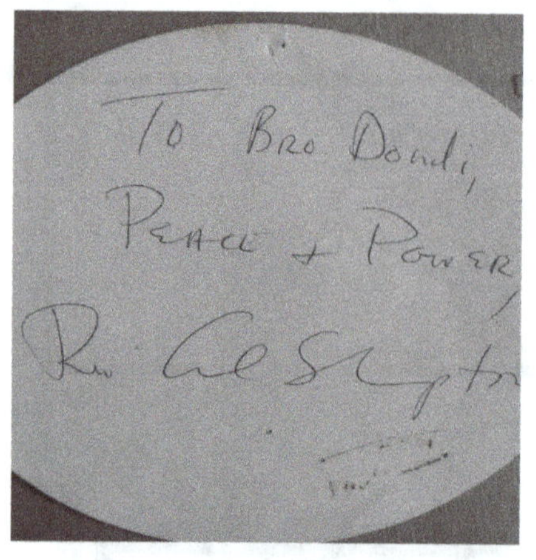

Al Sharpton took the time to sign this while we were at Sylvia's Restaurant with my students

Morgan State Crew

At the Million Youth March

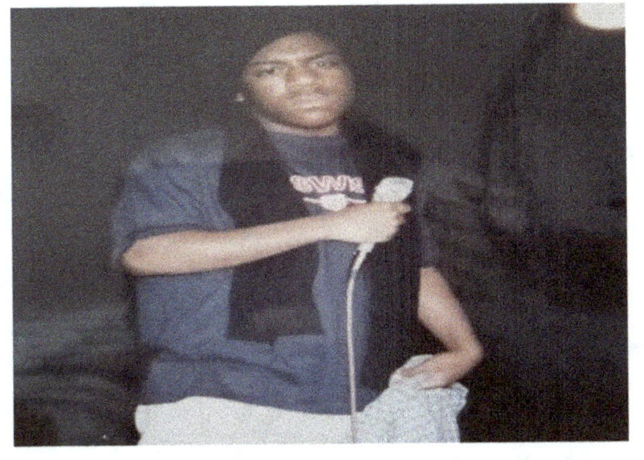

Student getting ready to perform on show

My Brooklyn connection Rapper Leschea

Me and Rerun at my
niece's wedding

Julio Receiving A certificate for speaking

FLEX Comedian

Cornell Scott From the Hill Health Center And Dondi Burroughs

Rerun supporting the Teens Only Show event

CITIZENS TELEVISION

Anissa Receiving a
community award

In front of Biggie Smalls after His Funeral

ONYX CREW

FIGHTING
AIDS
IN THE COMMUNITY

My boy Cool Aid on the show

Student performing on the show

Mike Jai White on show

Don B Reflective Wear

Before

Don B Reflective
Wear

After

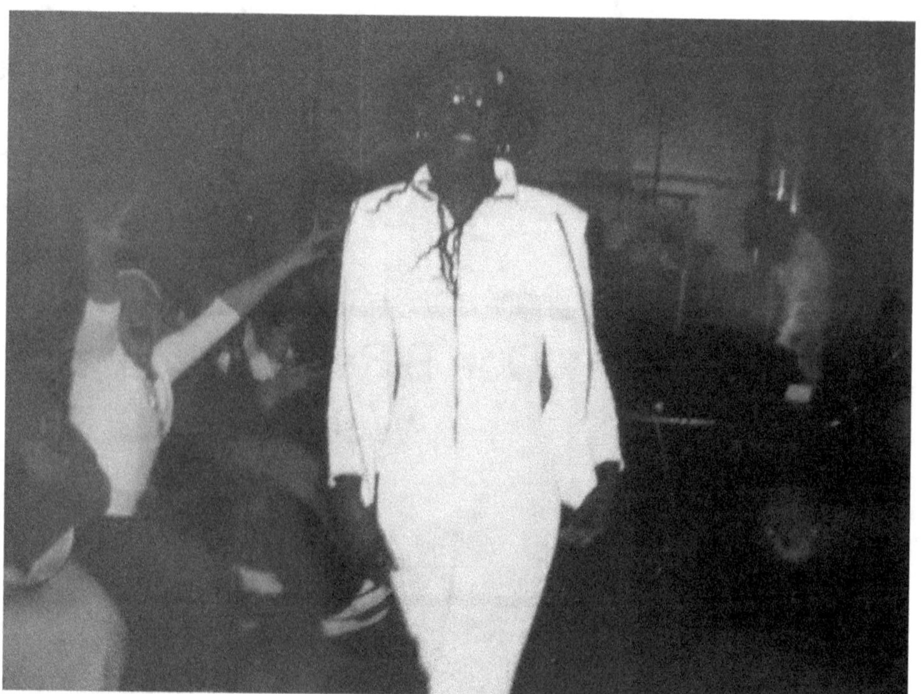

MILLION YOUTH MARCH

KRS 1 Dondi & Ms Melody

XZIBIT
Management Contact:
Suave (310) 821-0329
LOUD

·DON·B·
750 cc
MOTORCYCLE
APPAREL COMPANY

Tc Islam & Goddi

Dondi B & Tc Islam

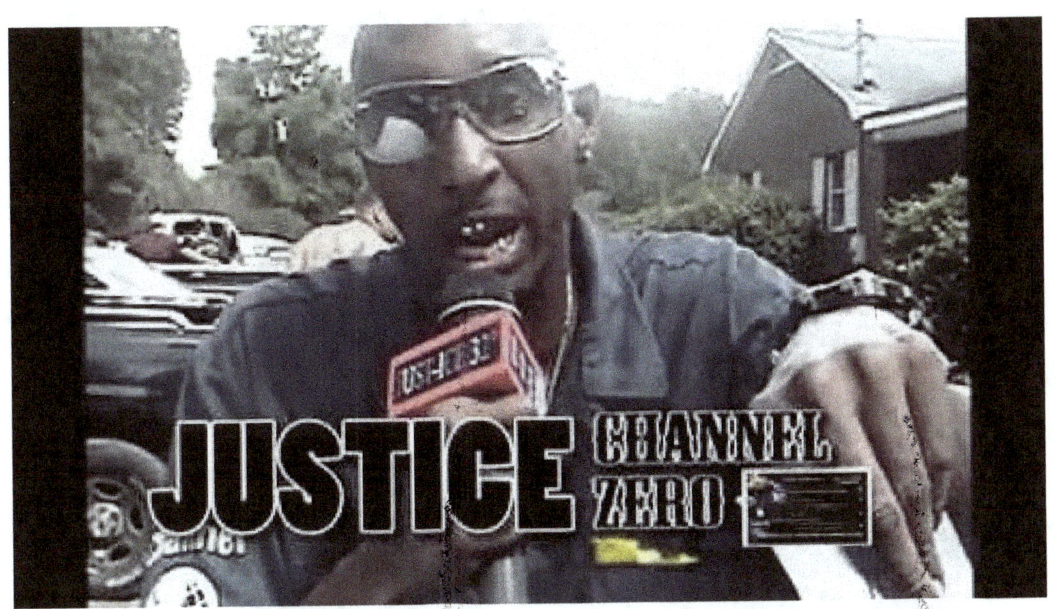

JUSTICE 32 DEGREEZ

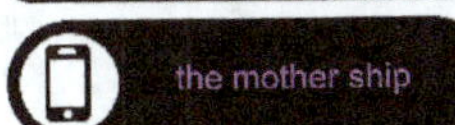

WWW.JUSTICE-32-DEGREEZ.MAILCHIMPSITES.COM

DONDI JOSE BURROUGHS

WWW.TEENSONLYTVSHOW1.MAILCHIMPSITES.COM